A CONSUMERS GUIDE TO SOUTHWESTERN INDIAN ARTS & CRAFTS

By Mark Bahti

Mark Bahti is a charter member and on the Board of Directors of the Indian Arts and Crafts Association. He has been a dealer of Indian arts and crafts for ten years, operating an Indian art shop in Tucson which his father, the late Tom Bahti, began almost a quarter of a century ago.

Mr. Bahti has been a judge at exhibits of Southwestern Indian arts and crafts and delivered many lectures on the subject. Like his father before him, his interest goes beyond the crafts to the Indian cultures that produce them and the problems affecting those cultures.

Photography by Marc Gaede

Marc Gaede, the photographer for this publication, has been actively taking photographs in the Southwest for the past fifteen years. He was a Marine Corps photographer from 1965-1968. For the last six years he has been the Chief Photographer for the Museum of Northern Arizona. In addition, he is the Staff Photographer for the Victorio Land & Cattle Company.

Mr. Gaede has an upcoming book on Anasazi Indian Ruins, consisting of his own creative photographs with a text by many well-known contributing authors.

Acknowledgements

We are very grateful for the help and cooperation given by the Museum of Northern Arizona. Dr. Hermann Bleibtreu, director of the Museum, granted the permission for use of the Museum's collections, greatly enhancing and expanding the publication. Marsha Gallagher, Ann Hitchcock and Helen Turner assisted by locating the materials from Museum collections. Mr. Ted Puhuyesva was very helpful in his donation of time as the demonstrator photographed drilling turquoise and putting on a bracelet.

Foreword

Indian art and culture are inseparable. Both have become the subject of intense interest as well as the focal point of considerable misunderstanding and misinformation.

The imitations, fads and misrepresentations plaguing Indian arts and crafts reflect, in a very real sense, what the tribes themselves are undergoing. It is the author's fervent hope that the cultures that produce these crafts will be able to continue to survive.

Perhaps those who have taken the time to learn more about true Indian arts and crafts will want to do the same for Indian cultures.

1975 by Bahti Indian Arts, 1708 E. Speedway, Tucson, Arizona 85719
Printed by Associated Lithographers, Inc.
3030 North 29th Drive, Phoenix, Arizona 85017

 ARTS & CRAFTS ASSOC.

The Indian Arts and Crafts Association is a national non-profit association with a current (late 1975) membership exceeding six hundred. Members include traders, museums, collectors, individual Indian craftspeople, tribal coops and guilds.

Its primary purposes include the promotion of Indian arts and crafts, development of a world-wide security system to reduce theft of Indian arts and maintenance of high ethical standards.

An important part of the IACA security program is a marking system which makes use of the National Crime Information Computer for faster, more efficient and wider coverage than any previous state or local program.

The IACA has been and continues to be active in introducing and supporting legislation that provides stiff penalties for misrepresentation of Indian arts and crafts.

Members are pledged to guarantee honest representation of any and all items they sell. Any member who, after a complete investigation of both sides, is found to be in violation of the IACA Code of Ethics, is ejected from the IACA. The information gathered is turned over to the appropriate authorities if there has been possible violation of federal, state or local law. (All complaints are handled on a confidential basis for the protection of both parties.)

Finally, the IACA acts as a clearing house for information that individuals, organizations or firms may request on Indian arts and crafts.

Further information may be obtained by writing the IACA, Box 367, Gallup, New Mexico 87301. (Phone 1-505-722-9488)

Baskets

Basket-making is the oldest of all the contemporary Indian crafts. Like rug-weaving it is so time-consuming that a weaver cannot really earn a living at it.

The primary reason that the craft still survives is that baskets remain important in both the everyday and ceremonial life of most Southwestern Indian groups. This has helped create a lively trade between groups which weave and those that do not.

The materials used in weaving a basket will not only affect the price in terms of the time involved in gathering and preparing the material before the actual weaving begins, but also in determining how well the basket will age.

Baskets woven of willow, for example, age very well, but willow is a difficult material to work with. Yucca is a good deal easier to use, but it does not age well. The green unbleached yucca and the white, bleached yucca will eventually fade and discolor.

The technique used to weave the basket is equally important in regards to the time and skill required. The wicker trays and plaques and baskets woven by the Hopi Indians of Third Mesa require more work than plaited yucca baskets they make, but not nearly as much work as the coiled baskets made by the Hopi on Second Mesa

In a plaited yucca basket, look to see how even the weave is and note the widths of the strips of yucca. The smaller the strips are the more time it took to weave the basket.

Many plaited yucca baskets have a geometric pattern, a figure or even a word woven into them. These designs, as with those on any other type of basket, should be judged on both the complexity of the design and how well it was woven.

In coiled baskets, the fineness of the yucca or willow used to sew the coils is an indication of the skill and time spent by the weaver. Similarly, the number of coils per inch is another important factor in judging the quality of a coiled basket.

The wicker and coiled baskets of the

Left: A yucca basket, faded and discolored with time.
Right: A willow basket, equally as old, has withstood the ravages of time.

Hopi plaited yucca baskets

Hopi coiled baskets

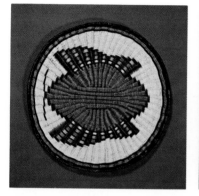 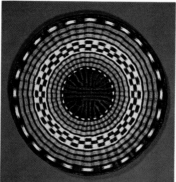

Hopi wicker baskets

Miniature willow baskets from 1½" in diameter

Hopi commonly utilize a surprizing number of different colors. Inspite of the many bright colors, most dyes are vegetal dyes. In certain instances, it is nearly impossible even for an expert to determine whether the dye used was vegetal or commercial, so the buyer should not be too concerned with the nature of the dyes used.

Color is a more important factor in Papago baskets in which black, white and green are most commonly used. Baskets employing red-brown, orange or yellow are seen less frequently and require additional work in gathering and preparing another weaving material. How much of the basket is stitched with the colored material will often depend upon its availability. During years when devilsclaw is in short supply due to drought, the costs of baskets using devilsclaw will be up and the quantity down.

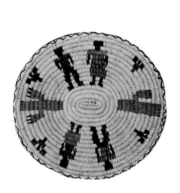  

Baskets with birds, animals or people woven into them will generally be more expensive not only because of the extra work involved, but also because the demand for them usually exceeds the supply.

Occasionally, Papago weavers will make baskets in the shape of such animals as owls, ducks, dogs, cats and rabbits. You should look for essentially the same things that you would in any other shape basket. If the head has been made separately as a sort of lid, look to see how well it fits. Because of the extra time and skill required to make these baskets, they will usually be more expensive than a conventionally-shaped basket of comparable size and quality.

Miniature baskets are not often made because of the extreme skill and tremendous amounts of time and patience required. A miniature of a two or three inch diameter may have more work in it than an average quality basket five times that size.

The horsehair baskets woven by the Papago are more commonly seen than the miniatures of yucca and devilsclaw. The reason for this is that it is not necessary to spend long hours gathering and preparing the material for weaving.

In order to weave a basket with a pattern, the weaver must have both dark and light horsehair. The latter is often hard to get. Several years ago, a rancher passing through found this out when his matching Palominos came up with matching haircuts.

In the split-stitch baskets woven by the Papago, the yucca does not entirely cover the bear-grass coils, requiring less time to weave such a basket. Depending upon the skill and inclination of the weaver, the stitching may be done in a simple straight-forward manner or be delicate and intricate enough to give it a lacey appearance.

Miniature horsehair baskets

Popular Myths

The fact that some basket designs have a "break" has nothing to do with "letting the evils spirits out". Rather it is done because the spiraling technique used in coiled basketry makes it impossible to weave a closed circle.

Care of Baskets

Try to display your baskets where they will not receive direct sunlight, as it may cause the colors to fade and the basket to become dry and brittle.

Avoid hanging them near the kitchen lest they absorb grease and smoke, discoloring them. If they get damp dry them immediately to avoid mildew.

If they are to be used as serving trays for fruit, bread or candy, it is advisable to use a napkin to line the basket. (Make sure you select a good stiff basket if you plan to use it for this purpose.)

Split stitch baskets

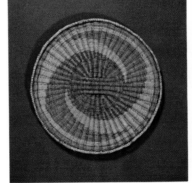

Old Hopi baskets

Weaving

A finely woven tapestry.

Handspun wool.

The weaving done by Navaho Indians is one of the most time-consuming of all native Southwestern Indian crafts. The loom must be built and the wool sheared from the sheep, washed, carded, spun and dyed before the actual weaving can begin. This means that a three-by-five foot Navaho rug of only average quality requires about 350 hours of work.

The first thing to do when purchasing a rug is to lay it out flat. Check for puckering or tightly curled corners. (If the corners are tightly curled they usually can be untied, loosened and then retied, but it can be tedious work.) Then fold the ends to the middle. This will help make evident any tapering or bowing of the rug. On a very large rug, a difference of an inch or so is neither noticeable nor important, but on a small, finely woven tapestry it is serious.

The finer the weave (the more warp and weft threads per inch) the more costly the rug as many additional hours must be spent spinning and weaving. How you intend to use the rug will be a factor in deciding how finely woven a rug you want. Clearly a more coarsely woven rug would be better suited for floor use than a finely woven one. Note too whether or not the quality and thickness of the weave is consistent throughout.

Commercially spun wool.

The warp threads, which essentially are the "bones" of the rug, may be of wool or cotton string. A rug with wool warps will hold up far better in floor use. The warp threads should not be visible. If they are it will be not only visually distracting but will also greatly reduce the life of the rug.

Check to see if commercially spun or handspun wool was used. Commercially spun wool will have a regular twist to it and upon close inspection the yarn will be seen to be composed of several smaller strands. Besides not wearing as well as handspun wool, rugs woven of commercially spun wool require less time to make and should therefore be marked as such and be sold for less than one of handspun wool.

While rugs using vegetal dyes require additional time spent collecting the plants and preparing the dye, therefore costing more, they are not inherently better than ones that utilize commercial or aniline dyes.

The colors used should be consistent throughout. If they are not it may be because the weaver did not dye enough wool and had to dye some more. In such cases it is impossible to match the colors perfectly. It can also happen if the weaver was careless in dyeing or carding and spinning the wool. The net result will be a mottled appearance at best or a patchy one at worst.

Popular Myths

The "spirit line" or "spirit trail".which is seen almost exclusively on Two Grey Hill type rugs is claimed to be woven in so the rug won't be perfect and "offend the gods". This is nonsense. Even the weavers do not agree on why they put it in. Their answers range from "to let the good spirits out" to "the tourists and collectors ask me to put it in."

There is no such thing as a ceremonial rug. While you may see rugs with yeis, yeibichai dancers or even sandpainting designs, they are never used in a ceremony.

Vegetal dye rugs are not "more authentic" than rugs that use commercial or aniline dyes. Aniline dyes have been around for over a century. By contrast most of the vegetal dyes used today were

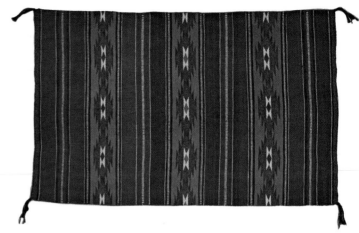

Vegetal dye rug.

Rug with mottled background.

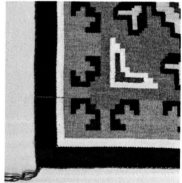

A "spirit line" in a Navaho rug.

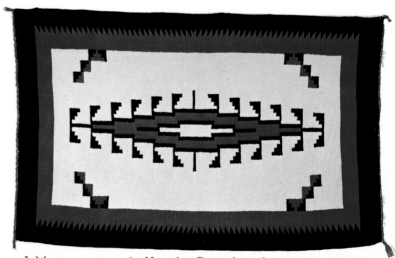

A Mexican copy of a Navaho Ganado style rug.

developed in the late 1930's.

At one time many areas produced distinctive styles, among them, Two Grey Hills, Teec Nos Pos, Wide Ruins and Ganado. In recent years these distinctions have blurred to the point where they no longer indicate the area where they were woven, but simply the style. Thus a Two Grey Hills rug may be woven near Ganado and a Teec Nos Pos far to the south in Window Rock.

Imitations

The most common imitations are those done in Mexico. By and large they are relatively easily spotted if one is careful. More than one experienced trader has accidentally purchased a Mexican rug from a Navaho weaver because he was in a hurry and only glanced at it.

Cut-a-way view of a Mexican rug.

The two main clues will be multiple warp threads along the edges and fringe at one end that was woven back under the weft threads to conceal it. Pushing apart the weft threads will expose either of these tell-tale signs.

An excellent booklet entitled *Are You Sure?*, published by the Navaho Tribe and the Museum of Navaho Ceremonial Art, covers this topic in depth for those who wish to pursue it further.

Chimayo rugs are often mistakenly believed to be of Indian origin. They are woven by the Mexican-American descendants of the early Spanish settlers in the Sangre de Cristo Mountains north of Santa Fe.

Care

A Navaho rug should be vacuumed periodically. Don't try to shake it out. The whipping action will fray and break the wool fibers. Floor rugs should be turned end for end and flipped over from time to time to insure even wear and mellowing of the colors. The same applies to those hung on a wall.

Besides vacuuming, a rug hung on a wall should be moth-proofed at least once a year. Should you store a rug, sprinkle it with moth crystals and then roll it up in order to avoid the creases you would otherwise have from folding it.

Floor rugs should always have a foam rubber pad underneath them. This will not only prevent them from slipping, but will also greatly extend the life of the rug. If you put the rug under an armchair or table you can expect to find four holes worn through the rug in a fairly short time.

Should you wish to hang your rug there are two excellent methods to choose between. The first method is simply a decorative wooden clamp which is made to fit the rug.

The second method involves mounting a strip of Velcro on the wall. The rug is pressed against it and the thousands upon thousands of tiny plastic hooks on the Velcro strip hold the rug. The rug can be repeatedly taken on and off with no damage to the rug.

When you need to have a rug cleaned always be sure and take it to an experienced cleaner. (Often the store that sold you the rug can recommend one.) Cleaners that handle fine Oriental rugs usually have the necessary experience.

Lastly, if your Navaho rug needs mending you might find yourself better off simply darning it with some store-bought yarn. Don't expect the Navaho who wove it to be able to repair it. Expert repair work requires another set of skills and techniques. Few are qualified and those that are charge sums equal to the great skill needed to do it, and they invariably have long waiting lists.

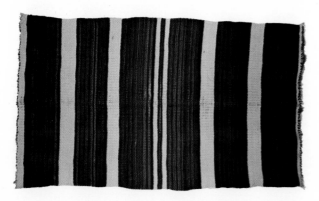

Kachina Dolls

The Hopi Indians are the only Pueblo Indians who still carve kachina dolls in any quantity. They are not dolls in the usual sense of the word. Instead, they are used to acquaint Hopi children with the many different kachinas.

Kachina dolls, carved from the root of the cottonwood tree, are representations of the kachina dancers, who impersonate the actual kachinas. A kachina may be the spirit of a plant, animal, place, object, insect or person.

Since the basic function of a kachina doll is to be a sort of "teaching aid", only a bare minimum of painting and carving is necessary. How far the carver goes beyond the basic distinguishing details is entirely up to him, his time and his skill.

The concept of the kachina doll is relatively new, going back just over a century. It probably stems from the kachina altar figures seen in the kivas, which served a different purpose.

Early kachina dolls were relatively plain and simple, but over the past fifty years or so the more elaborately carved "action kachinas" have become increasingly popular. The older style is not more authentic or better, it is simply another style.

The amount and degree of detail that can be added at the artist's disgression is tremendous. The arms, for example, may be indicated by a painted line, if at all. Taken to its extreme, it can be carved separate from the body, with even the fingers individually carved and painted, down to the lines on the knuckles.

As another example, the sashes or kilts may be painted on, carved in bas-relief, or carved separate or be painted cloth that was glued on. In the extreme, a sash may be handwoven in exactly the same fashion as the ones worn by the kachina dancer.

A very few carvers have become famous for being able to carve highly detailed kachinas out of single piece of cottonwood root. Most carvers make the arms, eyes, ears and accessories such as rattles out of separate pieces of wood that are then pegged and glued on. If the carver was careless in attaching them it will be readily apparent.

The degree of detail will be the most important single factor in determining the

An imitation kachina made of plaster-of-paris

A Navaho carving - not a true kachina doll.

price. Remember, a kachina doll that has a great deal of work in it is not a "better" kachina doll only a more expensive one.

Popular Myths

Contrary to a common story, carvers do not leave out some important detail when carving a kachina doll. The little differences between two kachina dolls or between one and the description in a book can be attributed to a number of factors. Usually it is due to the fact that a particular mesa or village may have its own variation of that kachina.

In this same vein it should be pointed out that the only difference between a Hopi kachina doll that is carved to sell and one that is given to a Hopi child is that one has a price tag and the other does not.

Imitations

Do not make the mistake of assuming that many kachina dolls may have been made on a lathe. A lathe can only make objects which are perfectly circular in cross-section, with no protrusions or irregularities. A kachina doll made on a lathe would more closely resemble a large, ornate pepper mill than a kachina doll.

About the closest thing to an imitation kachina doll that you are likely to run into are those which do not resemble any kachina doll, yet were carved by Indians. In most cases they are made by tribes which do not traditionally carve kachina dolls.

Care of Kachina Dolls

Avoid hanging a kachina doll under the vent of an evaporative cooler or some other humid spot as the paint may begin to blister and flake off. Too much direct sunlight can also be harmful as it will fade the paint.

Bugs may destroy not only the feathers or fur on a kachina doll, but some will actually attack the paint. To prevent this you can fumigate them or spray them with a good bug spray at a distance of not less than twelve inches.

If an arm or leg should break off, it can be put back by pegging it with a small brad or short length of toothpick and applying a drop of white glue.

Stone & Shell

Modern stone and shell jewelry is part of an unbroken tradition that extends far back into prehistoric times. Periodic trading expeditions to the Pacific shores and hours spent drilling, shaping, grinding and polishing remain virtually unchanged until the 20th century.

Even today a few craftspeople still use the old pump drills, though they are now equipped with modern drill points instead of stone points. The electric drill is not quite the time-saver one might imagine as care must be taken not to run them at too high a speed lest they heat up and crack the material being drilled.

Today it is primarily the Santo Domingo who still do stone and shell work. The

Each bead had to be individualy shaped for this necklace.

left to right: pipestone, shell, turquoise, olivella shell, serpentine, coral and Tortoise shell .

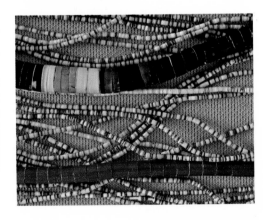

materials they use today come from all over the world. Coral, often thought of as an indigenous material, was first introduced by the Spanish and is now imported from Japan and Italy.

The quality of a heishe necklace ("hee-shee" from the Santo Domingo word for shell) is judged on a number of factors. The material used is one, with turquoise, ivory, tortoise shell and smooth, deep red coral among the more costly.

A fine quality heishe necklace should not have any rough edges or many chipped beads. A necklace composed of thick, poorly-finished beads that show a good deal of chipping should be an inexpensive necklace. On a well-made necklace the beads, regardless of their diameter, will feel smooth as you run the strand through your fingers.

The smaller the diameter of the beads and the more beads per inch, the more expensive the necklace will be. Those with as many as twenty-five or thirty beads per inch and diameters as little as three-quarters of a millimeter require tremendous skill, patience and time. The price can be expected to reflect this.

The birds, bears, turtles, fox and other animals that can be seen on a fetish necklace are not fetishes in the true sense of the word. They would be more appropriately labelled "carvings" since their purpose is ornamentation only.

(Fetishes have their origin in a Zuni legend about a time when certain gods turned all the animals to stone. Any object, however, may be a fetish, including plants, stones, shells or even an arrow point, as well as a carving. A spirit is believed to dwell in the object. The spirit, if treated properly, will provide supernatural assistance to the owner.)

This type of jewelry was begun over fifty years ago by a Zuni carver named Leekya who was encouraged by the well-known trader, C. G. Wallace.

The style of carving is not important except for the amount of work involved. One carver may be better known and therefore command a higher price than another, but it does not necessarily follow that his style of carving is better. It is largely a matter of personal preference.

Regardless of the style, the individual carvings should be smooth and free of obvious filemarks.

The degree of detail is up to the carver. The fetishes, particularly those done by some Santo Domingo Indians who have recently taken up the craft, may be simply crude silhouettes. A very few Zuni carvers may go to the other extreme, even putting in tiny bits of turquoise coral or jet for the eyes. (Look carefully, some prefer to use a dab of oil paint instead.)

Imitations

At one time Santo Domingo beadwork was so inexpensive that imitation was impractical. In the last couple of years that has changed and non-Indian beadwork has flooded the market. The imitations come from the Phillipines, Taiwan, Mexico, Japan and even the American Southwest.

For all practical purposes it is indistinguishable from the Indian-made product. Not surprisingly, then, it is often sold as Indian-made, both knowingly and unknowingly, by Indian and Anglo alike.

One clue to spotting the imitation can be the price. When you discover a necklace selling for a third or a fourth of what an Indian-made one normally sells for, it is a good bet that it is an imitation. The reason is that it is a seller's market for the Indian craftsperson, so he or she would have no reason to sell it to the store for far less than what it is worth.

Imitation fetishes are a little easier to spot. Each carver has a distinctive style. Even when an imitation is copied after the style of a particular carver, a knowleadgeable individual can usually spot the imitation. Shopping around and getting to know the names and styles of a few carvers will usually protect you from inadvertently purchasing an imitation for the real thing.

Popular Myths

Almost all of the coral necklaces one sees are, as they have been since they were first introduced into the Southwest by the Spanish, cut, drilled and polished by non-Indians.

Spiny oyster shell and a stone called argillite were the closest thing the prehistoric Indians in the Southwest had to a coral color. Contrary to an oft-repeated story, they had no coral before the Spanish arrived, and the coral used comes from coral reefs in the ocean, not "coral mines" as is sometimes claimed.

Care of Stone and Shell Work

Frequent contact with soap and water or oils may not only discolor a stone and shell mosaic, but also loosen the epoxy with which the stones were set.

With bead and fetish necklaces care should be taken not to allow them to hit anything. Simply leaning forward to look into a display case will cause the necklace to swing forward, striking the glass and chipping or breaking part of the necklace.

Whether the necklace is finished with silver catches, cones and beads or is simply wrapped in cotton string, as was done in earlier times, is a matter of personal taste. What it is strung on is of more importance. Avoid nylon monofilaments, non-braided strands of wire or cotton string as they will usually wear out and break faster. Waxed thread and dental floss should not be used as the knots may slip if the necklace is tugged or jerked. Braided nylon works very well and braided steel wire (called "foxtail") is excellent if the diameter of the hole in the beads is large enough. Light silver chains are not generally recommended as the links may weaken and separate.

Should you restring the necklace yourself with something other than wire or chain, use a dab of clear finger nail polish on the knots to prevent them from slipping. Be sure to leave a little slack when restringing or the necklace will not hang properly.

Zuni fetishes.

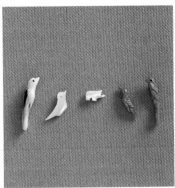
Imitation fetishes.

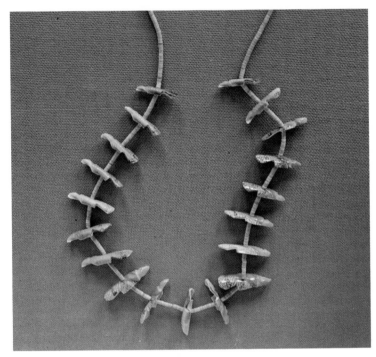
Santo Domingo fetish necklace.

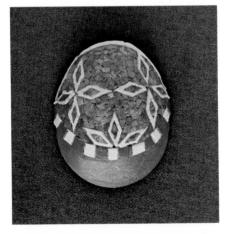
While giving the appearance of an imitation this is an older piece from Santo Domingo Pueblo, with turquoise and bits of plastic set on shell.

Turquoise

Turquoise is a hydrous aluminum phosphate colored by copper salts. It forms in a variety of types of rock. The rock in which it occurs is responsible for the markings or matrix in a piece of turquoise. The matrix may show up as thin black lines, brown patches, quartz crystals or even iron pyrite (Fool's Gold).

Similarly the color varies too, going from a light green to an intense blue, with literally dozens of shades in between. These variations in both color and matrix can occur within a single vein of one mine. This makes it impossible to positively identify the exact source of each and every piece of turquoise.

The cost of turquoise depends basically upon the current demand for turquoise of that particular color and matrix. It can range from a few pennies to many dollars per carat, with 140 carats to the ounce.

At present the most highly prized turquoise (and therefore the most costly) in the Southwest is a deep blue with a dark spiderweb matrix. It should be remembered that both color and markings are solely a matter of personal preference.

Almost all turquoise used in Indian silver jewelry is and always has been mined, cut and polished by non-Indians. The only notable exceptions are very early pieces of jewelry and Zuni jewelry. Even some Zunis, in an attempt to keep up with the demand for their jewelry, are using Persian-cut turquoise, called "snake-eyes", in their cluster and petitpoint work.

Turquoise from Iran, commonly referred to as Persian turquoise, has enjoyed increased usage and popularity in the Southwest over the past few years. The primary reason for this is that it is readily available, unbacked, in symmetrical shapes.

Most American lapidarists, in order to reduce waste, cut turquoise in free-form shapes. The stones are usually backed with epoxy in order to prevent them from cracking and breaking while being cut and polished.

Turquoise from the Royston Mine in Nevada

Persian turquoise from Iran.

Zuni Cluster ring set with Persian "Snake eyes"

Popular Myths

Green turquoise is not necessarily softer than turquoise of bluer hues. Pale, soft turquoise will turn a dark green over a period of time through constant use, but this has no bearing on turquoise that starts out green.

Through constant wear the stones in these pieces of jewelry have changed color. The variation in color of the center stone in the bracelet is due simply to a variation in the hardness in that stone.

There is no such thing as fossilised turquoise. Only plants or animals can become fossilised. Turquoise may be deposited in the cavities where the fossilised remains were dissolved out of the harder rock, but that does not make it a fossil by any stretch of the word.

While the price of turquoise is somewhat cyclical, people who claim to remember "the good old days" when top grade turquoise was cheap have faulty memories. For example, some of the turquoise taken from the Azure Mine in the Burro Mountains of New Mexico in 1893 averaged $5 per carat. By 1907 it reached a high of $25 per carat, over one hundred times more expensive per ounce than gold was at that time.

Perhaps in an attempt to help turquoise gain acceptance and popularity, a story began to circulate after the turn of the century to the effect that the prestigious Tiffany Company of New York owned the Cerillos turquoise mine near Santa Fe. The story was a complete fabrication. At one point Tiffany had to have a form letter printed up stating that they did not then own, had ever owned, or intended to own any part of any turquoise mine. Despite this the story persists to this day.

Persian turquoise is not new to Indian jewelry. It was first introduced in the late 1890's by Lorenzo Hubbell, trader to the Navaho at Ganado, Arizona.

A number of psuedo-experts would have you believe that stabilised turquoise is better than and different than treated turquoise. The fact remains that stabilising turquoise is simply one of the ways one can treat turquoise. This verbal smokescreen began as an attempt to avoid the negative feelings people have towards treated turquoise. Certain methods of treating turquoise enhance rather than section.)

The "copper" or "silver" you may see in some turquoise stones are actually nothing more than metal-colored epoxy used to fill in where soft matrix or a chip of turquoise once was.

Two types of epoxy were used to fill the stone in this ring. A third type of epoxy was used to back the stone. (This should not normally show on a finished piece of jewelry.)

Treated Turquoise

Treated turquoise has been around ever since it was discovered that its color could be altered. Both Indian and Anglo alike have been the victims and perpetrators. Grease, oils, paraffin and dyes have been used, but all affected only the surface. Besides often having a waxy or oily feel and appearance, in most instances the stone would "sweat" out the foreign substance on a warm day.

A piece of superbly crafted jewelry done by a well-known silversmith, yet set with treated turquoise.

Some dyes are applied for the sole purpose of darkening the matrix to make it stand out better and enhance the appearance of the stone.

A new technique of treating turquoise has been developed which utilises resins. This method has the distinct advantage of doing more than affect the color as it also hardens the soft, chalky, lower grades of turquoise to the point where they can be used.

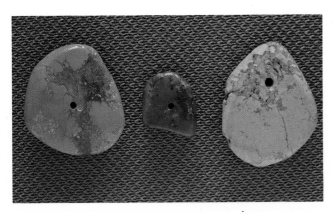

Left to right: Treated turquoise , treated turquoise with a blue dye added and untreated soft, chalky turquoise.

Turquoise treated in this manner is used by the Santo Domingo Indians for making most of their beads and nuggets. It reduces the amount of stone lost through breakage and enables them to sell the finished product at a fraction of what it would if good quality, hard, untreated turuoise were used.

Telling treated turquoise from untreated can be extremely difficult. If a bright blue dye has been added it will be readily apparent. Similarly resin filling a low spot on a nugget won't be hard to spot, but these are the most obvious examples.

You may be told that treated turquoise can be identified by touching the tip of your tongue to it. The theory behind this is that treated turquoise is not porous while untreated is supposed to be. Unfortunately for this "test", good, hard untreated turquoise is not noticeably porous.

Similarly, a glassy, mirror-like finish is no clue as a high sheen can be given hard untreated turquoise just as easily as treated turquoise.

Your best bet is to buy from a source that is both reliable and knowledgeable. Remember, though in most instances it will sell for considerably less than untreated

turquoise, there is nothing wrong with treated turquoise providing it is correctly represented as such.

Imitation Turquoise

Often thought of as a modern evil, imitation turquoise has been used in Indian jewelry since the late 1800's when bits of blue glass and trade beads were used in place of the costlier and harder to obtain turquoise.

An old bracelet made of brass and set with ceramic imitation turquoise.

Reconstituted or "reconstructed" turquoise first appeared in the 1940's. It is made by adding turquoise dust and chips to a plastic base, with a coloring agent sometimes being added.

More recently plastic imitations have appeared. Regardless of type or origin, most imitation turquoise manufactured since the 1930's has been set in machine-made jewelry.

A machine-made concha belt of nickel set with reconstituted turquoise.

A block of reconstituted turquoise.

Care of Turquoise

Untreated turquoise should never be allowed to come in frequent contact with soaps and oils as these will change the color to a dark green if the stone is at all soft or porous.

A very strong solvent, such as acetone will remove any soaps, oils or dyes in stone and most epoxy resins. Allowing the stone to soak up to 48 hours will drive out most of the foreign residues, returning the stone to its original color. (Allow the stone to dry away from any open flame and in a well-ventilated area.)

Pottery

How thin-walled the pottery is in relation to other work from that particular pueblo or tribe is an indication of the skill of the pottery and time spent in making the pot. The larger the pot, the more difficult it is to make, and thin walls make it just that much more difficult. (In carved ware, thin walls are impractical after a certain point.

Left: An unusually thin-walled bowl from Cochiti. Right: A thicker-walled, more typical Cochiti bowl.

The surface should be examined closely. In cases where a white clay slip is put on the put before the design is painted, as is done at Acoma, Zia and Cochiti, the thickness and evenness of the application should be noted. If it has been applied too thickly it may chip or flake off easily. If it has been put on too thinly or unevenly in some areas, the color of the clay beneath it will be visible.

Pottery from pueblos such as San Juan, Santa Clara and San Ildefonso usually have a polished surface. This is done with a smooth pebble before the pot is fired. A few potters spend many long hours polishing it in order to achieve a mirror-like finish.

Carved blackware from San Ildefonso Pueblo

The difference between the red and black polished ware from San Ildefonso and Santa Clara is due to different firing techniques rather than different clays. Both pottery types are made from the same clay and covered with a red clay slip. To keep the red finish, the pottery is fired in an oxidising atmosphere where the air is allowed to circulate freely, burning out any carbon deposits. To achieve a black finish the pottery is fired in a reducing atmosphere where no air is allowed to circulate and the pottery absorbs the carbon.

Firecloud on Hopi pot

Due to a combination of materials and techniques, pottery from some pueblos, notably the Hopi, may have "fire clouds". These fire clouds appear as smudges or discolored patches. How they affect the overall appearance and quality of a piece of pottery will depend upon the size, location and intensity of the fire cloud.

Examine the surface for cracks. Should you find one, tap the pot lightly with your

Acoma bowl showing spalling.

Mold-made pot with commercial paint

knuckle. If it rings the crack is nothing more serious than a surface crack, the merest fraction of an inch deep. If there is a dull "thud" instead then the crack goes all the way through and is a serious one.

Symmetry is much harder to achieve using the coil method instead of the potter's wheel, but a good piece of pottery should be reasonably symmetrical and not prone to rock and tip over at the slightest touch.

Regardless of whether the design is carved, modelled, incised or painted, it should be well laid-out and not show any signs of hesitation or unsteadiness.

Hopi pottery showing variations in quality

Lastly, some pottery, such as that from Acoma, is subject to spalling or pitting on the surface. This is due to the presence of gypsum in the clay which forms tiny crystals that exert pressure on the surface of the pot, popping out bits of the surface. This condition usually stabilizes within six months. While there are some precautionary measures that the potter can take to try and prevent this, there is nothing that can be done once the pot has been fired.

Imitations

Some of the pottery sold as traditional Indian handmade pottery is actually made on a potter's wheel, painted with commercial preparations and fired in a gas or electric kiln. This type of kiln firing almost completely eliminates the risk involved in firing in an outdoor kiln fired with coal, wood or manure.

Much of the brightly colored ware from Jemez and Tesuque pueblos is decorated with poster paints after it has been fired. In some cases it is not even fired but simply sun-dried.

Quite recently a number of pueblo potters have begun utilizing pots produced on a commercial basis from molds. Available in standardized shapes and sizes, they are being used not only in pueblos where traditional pottery has virtually died out, but also in pueblos that still produce great quantities of traditional handmade pottery. Many are glazed as well as painted with commercial paints instead of pigments derived from plants and minerals. There is nothing wrong with this providing they are represented correctly, which they often are not.

Pottery fired in an electric kiln will usually have no fire-clouding and will ring like fine china when tapped. Mold-made pottery will not only be perfectly symmetrical, but there may be a slight ridge running down the center of the pot. These, at best, are only general rules of thumb. The safest route is to further insure yourself by buying from a reliable source.

Popular myths

Pottery from some pueblos will have a break in the design around the rim. This is not there to "let evil spirits out" but rather is a design holdover from coiled basketry where the spiral technique made weaving a closed circle impossible.

The black ware from Santa Clara and San Ildefonso gets its color from absorbing the carbon during the firing process. It will not rub off.

Traditional Indian pottery is not any more or less fragile than most other types of ceramic ware.

Care of Indian Pottery

Most Indian pottery is fired at comparatively low temperatures, (usually not above 1300 degrees fahrenheit) making it porous. If you wish to use it as a planter, it is recommended that you use a glass jar as a liner. If this is not done, the surface will begin to "blister" and the pot will eventually be destroyed.

In order to prevent the bottom of the pot from marring the surface of a table or mantle you can make a felt pad to fit underneath the pot.

A Navaho cooking pot covered with pinon to waterproof it. Note fireclouding.

Left to right: Pottery from Taos, Picuris and San Juan made with mica-flecked clay.

Incised blackware from San Ildefonso Pueblo. Sometimes referred to as sgrafitto.

Silver Jewelry

There are so many types of Indian jewelry and so many different techniques and materials involved in its making that it is an area in which the consumer should exercise the greatest caution. Thorough familiarization with the type of jewelry you wish to buy and shopping around at a number of stores will help you avoid many of the more common pitfalls.

Sandcast Jewelry

Sandcast jewelry, done primarily by the Navajo, is cast flat in a mold carved from a relatively soft, heat-resistant material such as tufa, a volcanic sandstone.

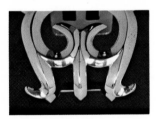

A barely visible hairline crack. (Center of photo)

A serious crack.

Check for any deep cracks in sandcast jewelry. Tiny hairline cracks can be expected in many rings and bracelets which have been hammered into shape. Deep cracks, however, are to be avoided. A good silversmith will fill any potentially serious cracks with silver solder. This "fill" will strengthen the bracelet, but it will show up on a tarnished piece of jewelry as the solder will tarnish more rapidly than the rest. If the silversmith has been careless in his use of the silver solder it can be distracting unless the piece is polished frequently.

Finally, check the finish. Some pieces of sandcast jewelry will have areas that were deliberately left rough and then oxidized (darkened) to heighten the contrast with the smooth, polished areas. If the silversmith has not taken enough time to properly finish the polished areas you will be able to see faint filemarks all over the surface. While a good finish can still be given such a piece it is a sign that the silversmith was less than conscientious.

Sandcast bracelet with a poor finish.

Note solder spot at top of pin.

Overlay

Overlay work, originally done only by the Hopi, is a technique also used by the Navaho. Contrary to an oft-repeated story, the design is not "carved" into the silver. Basically, the design is cut out of one sheet of silver and soldered to another. The recessed area is then oxidized for contrast.

Here you should look to see how well the design has been cut out. A wavering line or lop-sided design is an indication of an inexperienced or careless silversmith. The complexity of the design should also be taken into consideration. A design such as a coencentric maze pattern will make readily apparent even the slightest wavering of the line.

Almost all Hopi overlay work done in recent years is given a brushed finish with fine steel wool. Additionally, the recessed areas are textured with stampwork in order to further heighten the contrast and give the piece an added dimension. Recently, a few Navaho silversmiths have adopted these techniques.

An overlay pin showing a slightly wavering line.

Left: A Hopi pin.   Right: A Navaho pin.

Stampwork

Stampwork is most often done by the Navaho who may create a piece of jewelry using only this technique or use it in conjunction with another silverworking method.

Although it may not seem difficult, stampwork requires considerable skill and practice. If the stamp is not set flat on the silver before being struck, one edge may bite deeper into the silver than the other. At best this results in an unsatisfactory image or, at worst, a tear in the piece of sheet silver. If the stamp is held loosely or a glancing blow is struck, it may gouge the silver or create a double image. Finally, if the stamp is struck in the wrong place on the silver, nothing can be done to really "erase" it.

Besides showing poor spacing and double-images, solder has flowed into some of the stampwork.

Inlay Channel Work

The Zuni Indians do almost all of the inlay work you will see. The most important thing to check on this type of work is how well the stones have been cut and fitted. A piece made in a great hurry, with little care, will have stones that were so poorly cut that substantial amounts of metal-colored epoxy had to be used to fill in the gaps between the stone and the silver. Narrow gaps, however, should be of little concern as they are found in all but the very finest of pieces.

Next look at the surface of the stones. Often they will show signs of having been taken straight from the grinding wheel to the final polishing stage without any of the intermediate steps necessary to obtain a smooth finish and a high polish. These marks will often be emphasized by the dark polishing compound which will catch in the marks and grooves left by the grinding wheel or file.

Channel work ring with poorly-finished and poorly-fitted stones, one of which is chipped.

This piece has firescale over parts of the surface. It shows up as light purplish blotches. Care during buffing or proper finishing would have eliminated this.

Cluster Needlepoint Petitpoint

In the cluster, needlepoint and petitpoint jewelry, made by the Zuni, one should look for uniformity and symmetry in the size and shape of the stones as well as their settings. The great demand from a not-too-selective market encourages some craftspeople to cut stones of slightly irregular shapes and set them without taking the time to achieve a smooth, polished surface. Further, the bezels themselves may be poorly spaced and arranged.

An outstanding example of Zuni mosaic work.

Two very fine examples of Zuni inlay work.

Left to right: Examples of Zuni needlepoint, petitpoint and clusterwork.

From top to bottom: Navaho chip mosaic, a mosaic belt buckle of untreated Blue Gem turquoise and a Santo Domingo shell mosaic set with treated turquoise.

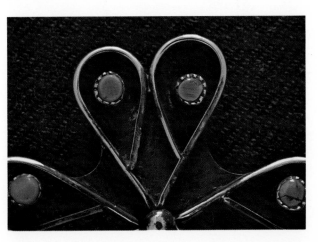

Liquid Silver

The Santo Domingo Indians create necklaces of handmade silver tubing. Usually referred to as "liquid silver", it is *not* made by pouring molten silver into tiny molds. Instead, sheet silver is cut into narrow strips which are then drawn through progressively smaller holes in a draw-plate until the strip becomes a tube. This tube is then cut into smaller sections. As a result, all handmade silver tubing will have a tiny, sometimes nearly invisible seam running the length of each bead. Unfortunately, machine-made tubing is now available which has such a seam too, so extreme caution is urged when buying.

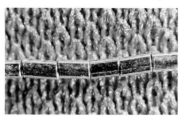

Though usually made of silver, brass and even gold are sometimes used. The tubing may be round, square or twisted, though the round tubing is far more common as it is considerably easier to make and is in greater demand.

The number of beads per inch is not quite as important as how well the necklace hangs. The strands should feel smooth and silky and, when worn, should live up to the name "liquid silver" in its appearance. When they do not hang properly it can be a matter of having been strung too tightly or strung on stiff cord, but usually it is

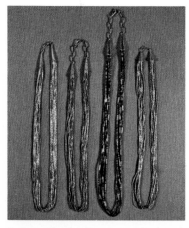

Left to Right: Square silver tubing, brass tubing, gold tubing with tortoise shell and square twisted silver tubing.

because the beads were poorly made.

Silver beads are worth taking an extra look at. Handmade beads are made from two silver discs that are hammered into hemispheres and soldered together. They may be plain, fluted or be decorated with stampwork. The seams should be soldered completely around and should be filed and polished. If they are not, they may be uncomfortable to wear.

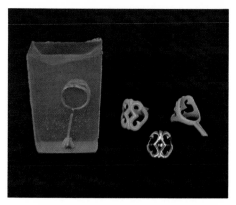

Because of the increasing demand for Indian jewelry and the considerable time and skill necessary to make silver beads, bench beads are becoming very common. There is nothing wrong with them as long as they are clearly labelled as such. They often can be spotted by a characteristic "shoulder" on each half of the bead.

Lost-Wax or Spin Casting

Although it is new to Indian jewelry, lost-wax casting is a very old jewelry-

Clockwise from the top the silver beads are: bench beads, handmade, bench bead, handmade, handmade (note how poorly made-both beads are soldered together and the two halves of each bead are not completely soldered.) and bench bead, as is the center bead.

Note tiny silver bubbles on this lost wax cast piece.

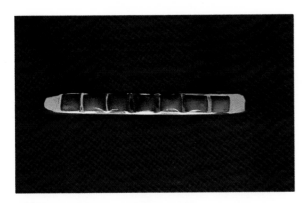

Lost wax cast channel bracelet set with dyed turquoise.

Examples of lost wax cast jewelry.

making technique going back many centures. Basically it involves making a wax model which is then cast in metal.

By making a rubber mold of an original piece of jewelry, countless wax models can be made which are then cast in silver. Originally it provided the Indian craftsperson with a way to both cut costs and meet the ever-increasing demand for Indian jewelry.

Since less time and skill are involved, the finished product should sell for less. Any silverworking technique used by the Indian can be exactly reproduced by this method. In fact, even a fingerprint on a warm wax model will show up on the silver casting. The result is that almost all lost-wax cast Indian jewelry made is not labelled as such or priced accordingly lower.

About the only readily apparent clue are the tiny little silver "bubbles" which form where air bubbles clung to the wax model when it was cast. They will usually show up in tiny corners and crevices.

There is nothing wrong with a piece made by the lost-wax method as long as it is priced and represented correctly and is Indian-made. A lost-wax cast bracelet that is simply polished by an Indian hardly qualifies as Indian handmade.

Much of the channel work done by Indians utilizes lost-wax cast silver frames that are made by non-Indians. The equipment necessary to produce rubber molds, wax models and the finished casting in quantity can be very costly and require another set of technical skills. As a result, most Indian silversmiths prefer to buy the finished casting regardless of who may have made it.

Imitations

The vast majority of imitation Indian jewelry comes not from Japan or any other foreign country, but rather is manufactured in the Southwest.

There are basically two types of imitation Indian handmade jewelry. The first is Indian-made but not handmade. This type of work began almost fifty years ago when Indians were hired to run hydraulic presses and punches to make inexpensive Indian jewelry for people who even then found the genuine handmade article too costly.

The machine-made imitation may run from the very obvious pot-metal and plastic to ones of sterling silver and turquoise. In a piece such as a concha, the whole concha is stamped out with one massive stamp. Each will be indistinguishable from the next. Any irregularity will show up on the same place on the next piece.

Most of the firms that produce this type of imitation make no attempt to pass it off as Indian handmade. The problem usually arises after the jewelry has changed hands several times.

This second type of imitation is handmade by non-Indians. This type of imitation was relatively unknown until the recent combination of increasing prices and demand made it feasible. Staggering amounts of this type of imitation is sold as Indian hand-made. Your only really sound protection lies in dealing with stores or individuals that are aware of the problem and have made a special point of going out of their way to insure that they do not inadvertently sell a non-Indian piece of jewelry as Indian-made.

Machine-made Zuni bracelet set with reconstituted turquoise.

The handmade concha in the center of the machine-made concha belt was made by the Navaho who owned it to replace the lost machine-made concha.

An Indian-made necklace with bench beads and treated Kingman turquoise of a type that is widely sold, usually advertised as having been heavily discounted.

Pawn Jewelry

The pawn jewelry you see in many stores is simply jewelry which was pawned by an Indian and was not redeemed within a year. Unredeemed pawn is referred to as "dead pawn". Originally, Indians used to pawn their jewelry either for a loan or simply for safekeeping in the trader's vault. Today a broke silversmith with an unfinished piece of jewelry or one that no one will buy, will often pawn it for what he can with no intention of ever redeeming it.

Machine-made jewelry, one of which is set with Lone Mountain Spiderweb turquoise.

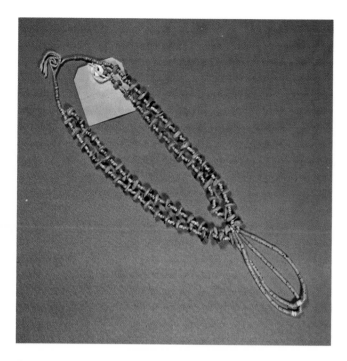

A unique piece - handmade of plastic and later pawned by an Indian who evidently couldn't afford the real thing.

A Word About Popular Myths

The designs you see on Indian silverwork can be stylized cloud, rain or bird figures, petroglyphs designs, animal forms or purely geometric designs. Though some may relate to a figure in a particular tribe's legends, they do not have such meanings as "safe journey", "courage", "strength" or the like. These "meanings" were attached to many symbols almost three-quarters of a century ago by non-Indians to help sell Indian curios and artifacts to the Eastern tourists who came out on the old Santa Fe Railroad. The myth that each symbol means something or that the designs tell a story persists to this day, perpetuated by Indian and Anglo alike.

Old jewelry is not inherently better than new jewelry. Just as there is junk being made today, so there was junk being made over a half century ago.

Similarly, pawn jewelry is not necessarily better - or very old - as is often implied. A poorly made piece of jewelry does not improve with age or a pawn ticket.

Additionally, some of the pawn jewelry you will see was never pawned. It is not unusual for someone to buy some pawn tickets, scribble on them and hang them on pieces of jewelry that have not been selling well. Also, a store may keep the dead pawn ticket when the piece is sold and "recycle" it.

Much of the Indian jewelry prior to about 1930 was made from American and Mexican silver coins. Contrary to stories you may hear, you cannot see the markings of the coins on items such as silver beads. The coins were melted down and hammered into a sheet before being made into beads. Beads made from two domed coins are relatively recent, having started about 1950.

Indian jewelry doesn't always meet people's notion of what it should be. Both the Zuni monogrammed napkin ring and the buttons made from an old pocket watch are over a half century old.

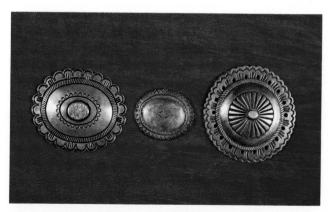

Old is not necessarily better. The well-made concha on the left is new. The poorly-made one in the center and the well-made one on the left were both made in the late 1800's.

Do not make the mistake that one eager collector did. He thought he had found a treasure in the form of a button made from a coin dated 1871. His enthusiasm faded somewhat when a museum curator explained that all the date meant was that it couldn't have been made before then - and that it was no guarantee it hadn't been made in 1971.

German silver is not silver but an alloy of copper, zinc and nickel used by some Plains Indian silversmiths. Indian silversmiths in the Southwest use sterling silver, which is 925 parts silver and 75 parts copper as set by law. An Indian silversmith seldom stamps his work "sterling" anymore than he would label his pottery "clay" or his moccasins "leather".

Care of Indian Jewelry

For keeping your Indian jewelry polished, a jeweler's rouge cloth is recommended. It should not be cleaned with silver dips or paste polishes as they can not only harm the turquoise, but will also remove the oxidation. Badly tarnished pieces can be cleaned by scrubbing them with a toothbrush and household ammonia. It should be rinsed afterwards with care being taken to avoid soaking the stones. (Most stones are set with a bit of cardboard or sawdust underneath to cushion it. The water will cause the cushioning material to swell, forcing the stone loose.)

If the oxidized area of a piece is removed, it can be re-oxidized by dissolving a bit of "liver of sulfur" (available in most drugstores) in water and applying it with a small paintbrush. Allow to dry before polishing.

If a stone falls out, it can be easily replaced. If it came out of channel

or inlay work, a drop of epoxy will do the trick. Otherwise just open the bezel up and, after making sure that there is some cardboard or sawdust cushioning the bottom of the setting, set the stone back in and close the bezel over the edge of the stone. (In the latter case it would not be a bad idea to take it to a silversmith as it can be a little tricky - too much pressure and you might break the stone.)

When you put on or take off a bracelet, make sure that you roll it on and off the inside of the arm, just above the wrist. If you don't you may inadvertently bend it a little each time, causing it to develop a crack and eventually break.

Shell, turquoise and coral will all burn at relatively low temperatures, so if your jewelry needs to be soldered, take it to a qualified jeweler. Otherwise you may end up with a burnt stone and the lame excuse "it must have been an imitation stone to burn like that."

Early silversmiths did not sign their work. Until the 1950's a signed piece was not a common sight. Today, with the development of individual styles and the demand of the customer to know who produced a certain piece, more and more silversmiths are signing their work. A number of silversmiths have used several different hallmarks, having replaced stamps that were lost, worn out or ones that they grew tired of.

FB	Fred Bowannie	⋏⋏	McBride Lomayestewa
J.A.	Jack Atakai	SFL	Sedalio F. Lovato
A⅁	Roy Anderson	Ⴑ	Glenn Lucas
V̶A	Videl Aragon	M	Mary Morgan
V A	Virgil Arragos	HN	Hoskie Nez
RLB	Robert Leonard Begay	JP	John Platero
KJB	Kee Jo Benally	H P	Herbert Platero
DTB	Dene Tsosie Bini	⑂	Elliot Qualo
JB	John Burnsides	ⓇR	James Roanhorse
△A⧸	Ambrose Lincoln	SR	Sam Roanhorse
⊢C	Henry Clark	P	Porfilio Shekeya
WC	Wesley Craig	M	Mike Simplicio
M D	Mary Dayea	⅁	Steven Sockyma
BD	Bennie Dickson	M⅁	Michael Sockyma
FE	Francis Eustis	R B	Roosevelt & Bernice Tekla
ᴚ	Juan Pedro Garcia	LT	Lorenzo Tortillita
⊬	Jimmie Herald	⬡	Roger Tsabetsay
ᕲ	Phillip Honani	B.TSO	Billie Tsosie
B H	Billie John Hoskie	⬥	Frank Vacit
H. IULE	Horace Iule	R̸	Roy Vandever
EJ	Eldon James	BW	Bryant Waatsa
⊼K	Chee Keams	T.K.W.	Tim K. Whitman
ᴚR	Jimmie & Rita King	DMY	Dick Mike Yazzie
-⊙-	Morris & Sadie Laahty	JDY	Joe D. Yazzie
₵	Curtis & Corraine Leekity	PY	Pat Yazzie
C L	Charlie Lewis	RHY	Richard Henry Yazzie
ⅼⅼⅼ⤬⤬━	Charles Loloma	⅁Y	Gary Yoyokie

Before You Buy

Hopefully this booklet wll not only aid you in spotting imitations, but will also serve to help you determine whether or not an item is of good quality. Do not expect an inexpensive item to meet high standards. The price should reflect the degree of quality and this booklet can assist you in making sure that it does.

Disregard discounts and their size and number. The important thing is the price you paid, not the price you didn't pay. See what the price is when the dust settles. The claimed "normal" retail price may be so unrealistically high that even a fifty or sixty percent discount might be just barely enough to bring the price back down to where it ought to be. Shopping around and knowing what you are buying will help you decide whether a discount is genuine or not.

Beware of the "real deal". You may find yourself buying stolen goods, junk or an imitation. Currently it is a seller's market. A good Indian craftsperson never lacks a market for quality work.

A good example of this is three Navaho ladies whom I encountered at a trading post on the southern edge of the Navaho Nation. They had not only their own weavings, but that of two relatives as well. That day I was to see them three more times at three different trading posts. In all, they went to five trading posts, taking bids, before selling to the highest bidder. They knew how much they wanted for their weaving and they knew they could get it, which was exactly what they did.

Certain craftspeople have developed widespread reputations for their work. It may be based on a distinctive style, a new technique, revival of an older style or technique or simply very good public relations. Whatever the cause, their work can be very expensive.

"Reservation made" is a meaningless phrase. A piece of jewelry is not more or less authentic just because of where the craftsperson was when it was made. Similarly, "reservation direct" is an empty phrase.

Special offerrings of Indian crafts deserve special attention. To protect yourself against unscrupulous fly-by-night crooks masquerading as travelling traders, find out *before* you buy who guarantees what you plan to buy. Usually the sponsoring store does not, passing the responsibility on to the people running the offering. Get it in writing, along with any representations the salesperson may have made, on the saleslip and get it signed.

Regardless of where you buy, it is wise to have all representations in writing. This will not only serve to protect you from over-eager and misinformed salespeople or deliberate fraud, but will also be helpful to both established and budding collectors.

Should you be one of those determined to buy primarily for investment make sure that you buy items you, personally, like. Buying in this fashion will assure you that even if the investment aspect pans out, you will not be stuck with an ugly reminder.

Where to Buy

This probably is one of the trickier things to do when buying Indian arts and crafts: finding a reliable, knowledgeable and honest source.

One can buy from those who have been in business many years. This will help you avoid fly-by-night operations, but it is more a guarantee of durability than reliability.

The Indian Arts and Crafts Association is an excellent place to check with before buying. Besides advising you of helpful publications, they will provide you with the names of all IACA member stores in the area where you plan to buy.

The local Chamber of Commerce is a good place to start. The names they give you can be cross-checked with the Better Business Bureau. Museums are also very fine places to inquire after the names of reputable shops.

Museum gift shops are good places to shop as are tribal enterprises such as guilds and cooperatives, particularly for the crafts that that particular tribe makes.

Buying "direct from the Indians" can be an enjoyable experience, it is no guarantee that you are buying it for less. The Indian craftsperson is fully aware of what the retail prices are for his craft elsewhere.

Remember too that the complexion or cultural heritage of the seller has no bearing on the merchandise's authenticity or lack of it.

An Indian-sounding name for the store and Indian-style decor may create a quaint and colorful atmosphere, but that doesn't mean that the goods are Indian-made. Heishe, concha belts, fetishes, squash blossoms and the like can be made by non-Indians as easily as by Indians. Don't assume - *ask*.

After You Buy

Please do not go into a store with the attitude that they are going to cheat you. Be a wise, cautious buyer, but remember that our legal system says a person is innocent until proven guilty.

If you ask if a piece is genuine and you are told that it is, don't repeat the same question about the same piece a moment later. If the person is honest you will only insult them. If the person is dishonest, it is unlikely that they will suddenly break down and confess.

Should you suspect that an item you purchased is not what it was represented to be, try and get a few opinions from other stores. Then go back to the store where you purchased it. Explain the problem calmly and quietly. It may have been an honest mistake that can be quickly and easily settled to everyone's satisfaction.

In the event that the matter is not resolved to your satisfaction, contact the nearest Consumer Protection office. If the suspected offender is a member of the IACA, contact that organization. Hang on to your receipt and the item in question. Keep track of whom you talked to, when and what was said. Important correspondence should be xeroxed and sent registered mail.

Then stick with it until the problem is settled. If you don't act when you have been defrauded you make it that much easier for the same thing to happen to the next person who comes along.

General Comments

Yes, Indian arts and crafts used to cost less, but then so did almost everything else. The big reason for the increase is that the Indian craftsperson has adopted our economic way of life, and that automatically includes our much higher cost of living. In any event, don't ask what the Indian was paid unless you are in the habit of asking the car dealer what the auto worker was paid or the waitress what the cook was paid.

Indian art is constantly changing, from within and without, incorporating some ideas, rejecting others, but with the result always being unmistakably Indian.

The newer types and forms of Indian arts and crafts are not discussed in this booklet as they are not widely available and, like paintings, verge more into individual art rather than a tribal craft. Where this happens individual and collective personal preferences play the greatest roll, and they have no place in a factual guide.

"It's nice but it isn't Indian" and "But it's not traditional" are comments often made by well-meaning patrons when viewing contemporary Indian arts and crafts. While anyone interested in Indian arts and crafts is insistent on the importance of it maintaining an Indian flavor, it is wise to remember that what was labelled "non-traditional" fifty years ago is now referred to as old-style, traditional work. So don't write off modern Indian art simply because it is labelled "non-traditional".

In a similar vein "outside influences" and the "evils of commercialization" are claimed to rob the crafts of their authenticity. There is serious doubt whether any craftsperson ever created in a cultural vacuum. In the case of Indian silversmithing, "outside influences" from Hispano-Mexican sources were responsible for the inception of the craft. Further, the Indian craftsperson must create an item for which there is a market or starve. Unfortunately many collectors will still ask "Is it traditional or was it made just to sell?" It would be difficult to find a craftsperson who worries whether the customer for his craft will be Indian or non-Indian.

Recommended Reading

Adair, John. *The Navaho and Pueblo Silversmiths.* University of Oklahoma Press. Norman, Oklahoma. 1944.

Bahti, Tom. *Southwestern Indian Arts and Crafts.* K. C. Publications. Las Vegas, Nevada. 1966.

Bahti, Tom. *Southwestern Indian Tribes.* K. C. Publications. Las Vegas, Nevada. 1968.

Bedinger, Marjorie. *Indian Silver.* University of New Mexico Press. Albuquerque, New Mexico. 1973.

Bennet, Noel. *Genuine Navaho Rug-Are You Sure?* The Museum of Navaho Ceremonial Art. Santa Fe, New Mexico. 1974.

Branson, Oscar. *Turquoise: Gem of the Centuries.* Treasure Chest Publications. Santa Fe, New Mexico. 1975.

Colton, Harold S. *Hopi Kachina Dolls.* University of New Mexico Press. Revised ed., Albuquerque, New Mexico. 1959.

Conroy, Kathleen. *What You Should Know About Authentic Indian Jewelry.* Gro-Pub Group. Denver, Colorado. 1975

Dedera, Don. *Navaho Rugs.* Northland Press. Flagstaff, Arizona. 1975.

Dutton, Bertha. *Navaho Weaving Today.* Museum of New Mexico Press. Santa Fe, New Mexico. 1961.

Dutton, Bertha P. *Indians of the American Southwest.* Prentice-Hall Inc. Englewood Cliffs, New Jersey. 1975.

Kent, Kate Peck. *Navaho Weaving.* Heard Museum. Phoenix, Arizona. 1961.

Lamb, Dr. Frank W. *Indian Baskets of North America.* Riverside Museum Press. Riverside, California. 1972.

Lambert, Marjorie F. *Pueblo Indian Pottery.* Museum of New Mexico Press, Santa Fe, New Mexico. 1966.

Maxwell, Gilbert. *Navaho Rugs, Past Present and Future.* Desert Southwest Publishing. Palm Desert, California. 1963.

Neumann, David L. *Navaho Silverwork.* Museum of New Mexico Press. Santa Fe, New Mexico. 1971.

Newman, Sandra Corrie. *Indian Basket Weaving.* Northland Press. Flagstaff, Arizona. 1974.

Northrop, Stuart. *Turquois and Spanish Mines in New Mexico.* University of New Mexico Press. Albuquerque, New Mexico. 1975.

Seven Families in Pueblo Pottery. University of New Mexico Press. Maxwell Museum of Anthropology. 1974.

Woodward, Arthur. *Navaho Silversmithing.* Northland Press. Flagstaff, Arizona. 1972.

Wormington, H. M. and Neal Arminta. *The Story of Pueblo Pottery.* Denver Museum of Natural History. Museum Pictorial No. 2, 1951.

Wright, Barton and Road, Evelyn. *This Is a Hopi Kachina.* Museum of Northern Arizona. Flagstaff, Arizona. 1962.

Wright, Margaret. *Hopi Silversmithing.* Northland Press. Flagstaff, Arizona. 1972.

Inside back cover: Vera Pooyouma has been weaving wicker baskets for over a half of a century.